People of the Bible

The Bible through stories and pictures

The Trials of Daniel

Copyright © in this format Belitha Press Ltd, 1985

Text copyright © Catherine Storr 1985

Illustrations copyright © Geoff Taylor 1985

Art Director: Treld Bicknell

First published in the United States of America 1985
by Raintree Publishers Inc.
330 East Kilbourn Avenue, Milwaukee, Wisconsin 53202
in association with Belitha Press Ltd, London.

Conceived, designed and produced by Belitha Press Ltd,
2 Beresford Terrace, London N5 2DH

ISBN 0-8172-2040-2 (U.S.A.)

Library of Congress Cataloging in Publication Data

Storr, Catherine.
    The trials of Daniel.

    (People of the Bible)
    Summary: Retells the Old Testament story of
Daniel's unswerving faith in God, even in a den
of lions.
    1. Daniel, the Prophet—Juvenile literature.
2. Bible. O.T.—Biography—Juvenile literature.
[1. Daniel, the Prophet.   2. Bible stories—O.T.]
I. Title.   II. Series.
BS580.D2S76   1985   224'.509505   85-12288

ISBN 0-8172-2040-2

First published in Great Britain in hardback 1985
by Franklin Watts Ltd,
12a Golden Square, London W1R 4BA

Printed in Hong Kong
by South China Printing Co.

 23456789   89 88 87 86

The Trials of Daniel

Retold by Catherine Storr
Pictures by Geoff Taylor

Raintree Childrens Books
Milwaukee • Toronto • Melbourne • London
Belitha Press Limited • London

Nebuchadnezzar, the King of Babylon, laid siege to the city of Jerusalem. After he had won the battle, he took many of the Judean children as hostages, back to Babylon.

He ordered Ashpenaz, one of his servants, to choose four young boys from among them. They were to be fed on special meat and wine to make them grow strong and good-looking. Ashpenaz chose Daniel, Shadrach, Meshach, and Abednego.

Daniel asked Melzar, who looked after the boys, "Let us eat beans and drink water, as our God commands. You will see that we shall grow up as strong as the others who eat meat and drink wine."

Melzar was frightened of the King's anger, but he liked Daniel, and he agreed that they should try. After ten days, when he saw that Daniel and the other three boys were still strong and healthy, he allowed them to go on eating and drinking the food which was ordered by their God.

The boys grew in all skills and learning, and Daniel, especially, understood visions and dreams. In the years that followed, the King found them ten times wiser than his magicians and astrologers.

Now Nebuchadnezzar dreamed a dream. He sent for his wise men and his magicians. "Tell me what I dreamed and explain to me what it means," he said.

They said, "O King, live forever! No one can
tell you what you dreamed. Tell us what your
dream was, and we will tell you what it means."
Nebuchadnezzar said, "I can't remember the dream.
Tell me about it, or I will have you cut to pieces."

The wise men and the magicians were terrified. Arioch, the captain of the King's guard, was sent to kill them.

But Daniel said to him, "Do not kill the wise men. God has told me the King's dream, and what it means."

When he came before the King, Daniel said, "You dreamed that you saw a great image, which was very bright and very terrible. Its head was of gold, its breast and arms of silver, its belly and thighs of brass, and its legs of iron. Its feet were part iron, part clay.

"A stone burst out of a mountain. It hit the image which broke into pieces, and became dust. The wind carried the dust away. This means that there will be four kingdoms after yours. Your kingdom is the first and is like the head of gold. The last will be like the feet of iron and clay, partly strong, partly weak, and will break. Then God will found another kingdom which will never be destroyed."

Nebuchadnezzar said, "Daniel's God is God of gods." He made Daniel a great man and a ruler in Babylon.

13

After this, Nebuchadnezzar made a huge golden image on the plains of Dura. He called together all the princes, the governors, the captains, the judges, the treasurers, and rulers.

A herald proclaimed, "When you hear the sound of the cornet, the flute, the harp, the sackbut, psaltery, dulcimer, and all other kinds of music, you must fall down and worship this golden image. Anyone who does not obey this law will be cast into a burning, fiery furnace."

Nebuchadnezzar sent for the three young men and said, "Why don't you worship my gods or the golden image? If you do not, I shall cast you into a burning, fiery furnace."

Then Shadrach, Meshach, and Abednego said, "O Nebuchadnezzar, we cannot worship your gods. Our God can deliver us from the burning, fiery furnace. But even if he does not, we will not serve your gods or worship them."

Nebuchadnezzar was furious and commanded that they should be bound and cast into the furnace.

But he looked and saw them walking in the middle of the fire. Their clothes were not burned, nor their hair singed, and there was a stranger with them who looked like the Son of God.

The King said, "Blessed is the God of these young men. He has delivered his children from the fire. No one shall speak against this God."

Now Nebuchadnezzar had another dream. He saw a great tree, reaching from earth to heaven, with birds in the boughs and beasts in the shade.

But a watcher, a holy one, came from heaven and cried, "Cut down the tree, shake off the leaves, and scatter the fruit. The King shall be wet with the dew from heaven, and his heart shall be changed to a beast's heart."

Daniel was troubled. He said, "You are the tree, O King. Your enemies will drive you out of your kingdom. You will dwell in the fields and eat grass like the beasts until you acknowledge that my God is the Lord."

Nebuchadnezzar died, and Belshazzar
became the next King of Babylon. He made a
great feast for a thousand lords.

He took the sacred golden cups from the temple of Jerusalem, and he and his guests drank from them. They praised the gods of gold and silver, of iron and of wood and stone.

Suddenly, Belshazzar saw the fingers of a man's hand writing some strange words on a wall. They wrote, MENE, MENE, TEKEL, UPHARSIN.

The King was troubled. He promised his wise men fine clothes of scarlet, and golden chains, if they could tell him what this meant. When they could not, the Queen said, "Daniel is cleverer than these magicians. He understands dreams and omens."

Daniel said, "O King! God gave your father his kingdom. But when he grew proud, God took his kingdom from him. The writing means, MENE: God will destroy your kingdom. TEKEL: You are weighed in the balance and found wanting. UPHARSIN: Your kingdom is divided and given to the Medes and Persians."

That night, Darius, King of the Medes, killed Belshazzar and claimed his kingdom.

Darius set three presidents to rule over the many princes of the kingdom. The first of these was Daniel. The other presidents and princes wanted to get rid of Daniel. They tried to find something he had done wrong, but there was nothing.

They said to Darius, "O King, live forever! Make a law that no one is allowed to pray to a god or to ask for a favor from anyone except from you. If any man does not obey this law, he shall be cast into the den of lions."

King Darius agreed. He signed a royal statute and bound it with the laws of the Medes and Persians, which were not to be broken.

Daniel knew of this law. But he was determined to pray to his God as he had always done. He opened his window, which looked toward Jerusalem. He kneeled there three times a day and he prayed.

The presidents and princes saw Daniel
praying at his window, and they told the King.
"You must keep your word," they said, "and
cast Daniel into the den of lions."
Darius was miserable.

He loved Daniel, and did not want to hurt him. But he could not go against the law of the Medes and the Persians.

He told his guards to cast Daniel into the den of lions. Darius, himself, sealed the stone guarding the entrance to the den, with his own seal.

Early the next morning, the King went to the den of lions. He called out, in a sad voice, "O Daniel, servant of the living God, has your God saved you from the lions?"

Daniel replied, "O King, live forever! My God sent his angel to shut the lions' mouths, and I am unhurt."

Then Darius was glad. His servants brought Daniel out of the lions' den. And his enemies were thrown to the lions instead. Darius wrote to the people of all nations, saying, "All men shall tremble before the God of Daniel, for he is the living God."

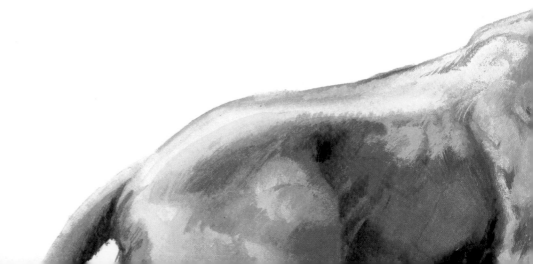

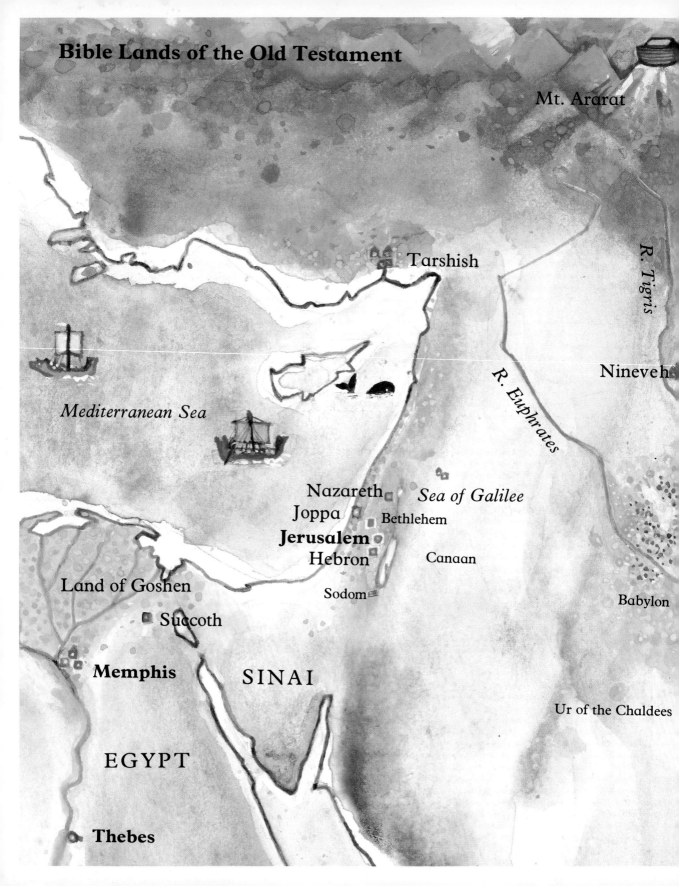

Bible Lands of the Old Testament

Mt. Ararat

Tarshish

R. Tigris

Nineveh

R. Euphrates

Mediterranean Sea

Nazareth

Sea of Galilee

Joppa

Bethlehem

Jerusalem

Hebron

Canaan

Land of Goshen

Sodom

Babylon

Succoth

Memphis

SINAI

Ur of the Chaldees

EGYPT

Thebes